BLAMEFOREST

JASON STOCKS

Published by Mindstir Media, LLC
45 Lafayette Rd | Suite 181| North Hampton, NH 03862 | USA
1.800.767.0531 | www.mindstirmedia.com

Printed in the United States of America

ISBN-13: 978-1-7368000-0-0

My sense of the past is vivid and slow.
I hear every sign and see every shadow.

—Barry Hannah, "Water Liars"

For Kenny and Lucia

Contents

ONE:

the future is in the past

Greenacres My Ass

Saturday night
Walking home from the store
When four shots popped off.
Around the corner
Two brothers lay dead
With holes in their heads.
I almost stepped on 'em.
They weren't so awkward
And out of place that they
Didn't look like they belonged.
But like, laying there, slightly fetal,
Sleeping peacefully,
Is what they were born to do.

The blood puddled.
Ha, it was part of the act.
"Hey fellas," I said,
"Wake the hell up.
Are you drunk? What?"

The night was warm.
It felt good to be outside.
Could just barely perceive the brine
From the nearby beach
Over the humid aroma
Of blood and gunpowder and piss.

When the police came
With all their flashy lights
And crew cuts
I was still there,
Standing over them.

Talking to them.
Mesmerized
By the loss of life
So close to my home
In Boca Raton.

The cops said freeze.
I was already froze.
They said don't move.
I couldn't, didn't want to.
The noise they made was petty
Like betting on a boxer
You know will lose
Because you think he's a swell dude.

One of the dead bodies was smiling
A snow-white smile.
His momma don't know he dead yet.
He won't be smilin' then.
She'll whoop his ass,
Especially if she black.

A white mom
Like mine
Might swallow some pills,
Cover her face with a pillow
And take her own life. Nah,
She'd shoot my dad
And his young Colombian wife.

In the papers they'll say it had to do with drugs.
A deal gone wrong and someone turned the tables on 'em.
But it won't be that they were the victims
Without having deserved it.
No sir, they will be *thugs* in death.
The public will feel it was justified

And everyone feels better,
Safer.
Sure, we'll avoid the bloodstains
For a few days, but before long
Kids'll be doing hopscotch
Over the tainted area again.
Their deaths will become whispers
Between affluent parents
Who know they haven't seen
Or heard the last of it.

The news said one was 17.
The other brother was younger.
They didn't live here.
We felt better, but not for long.
Gunshots rang out last night
And the guy doing the shooting was white.
He screamed at all us losers
Saying "Die! Cowards! Die!"
And I, well I took my baby inside and began to cry
For the parents whose kids lost their lives.
The apartment people tryin' to hide it too.
They have money to make I guess
And stuff like this is such shitty publicity.

And on a playground for fuck's sake.

The manager and her assistant
Came out early next morning, as the sun was coming up
To remove the crime scene tape, and spray
Chalk, blood and piss off the sidewalk.

The reporters, trying to get a story
Worried us. They worried us.
Writing things down like they're still in college
Or fresh out, excited about having gainful employment.

Talking to them, their anxious, accountant eyes, was like
Lying on our taxes and being busted by the IRS.

We waved 'em off, like mosquitoes.
Our privacy had been invaded.
We waved 'em off, like fat-cocked Florida skeeters.

The po-lice, pleading with us to tell the truth
About what we knew
Were troublesome fucking pigs
We didn't have to answer to.

So we didn't.

Game Changer

When I was a kid I thought
Changing my name would change
Who I was, where I was born and grew up.
I wanted to be called Bo or Luke Duke
And be raised by a silver-haired sage in overalls.
Would'a had a fast ride, like a '69 Charger
To haul my moonshine, late nights, some
Isolated dirt-road town. Wanted a fine-ass
Cousin 'round the house who
Wore short shorts all the time.
Who had her fine-ass friends over all the time
(Spied on while undressing
After returning home from the swimming hole).
Loneliness was replaced by horniness
In my poor little lonely-boy mind.

I believed, that if I changed my name
It wouldn't be my parents who had me
But a rich family, who had a brick house
In Clinton, Mississippi. No doubt
I would've tried out for the select soccer club.
Would've gone to private school in the country.
Would've been called Colby, or Macaulay probably,
Broad-shouldered, square-jawed
And not so skinny my bones showed underneath my clothes.
Might've gone to Ole Miss, straight away
Instead of workin' a decade at the rendering plant
Where dog food is made.
Where I always come home from
Smelling like who and what I am.
That ain't doin' me any favors either.

If I could've changed my name
Think I would've settled on Reese.
Knew a dude named Reese from Russellville.
He played quarterback for the Cyclones.
His sister was a cheerleader, prom queen.
Both parents were attorneys. We thought they had it all.
Their house was always prettiest during Christmas, all electrified
And jubilant. But Reese shot his mother and father in the head
With a .357 while they slept,
And hung his 7 year old sister
And himself with a chain in the basement.

After an invasive investigation
They were buried in the weeds at Rest Haven.
Their names and faces faded from the papers.
Bringing the incident up was a big no-no.
The house sold. To a sweet young family from Tupelo, and folks moved on.
History became myth, making the ghost stories, told in that valley—
When the leaves go from green to yellow to red—
Worthless, my old man always said, as tits on a witch.
As if we're programmed to forget shit.

Manslaughter

That thing inside me
that keeps up with time,
feels like a brick wall
hit by a car driven by Vince Neil.

My eyelids *feel* like Mick Mars' face *looks*.

I only want to drink
and smoke
and never let my head go
to that place ever again.

I want, I need
to say ugly grotesque things
to people who
can't see the forest for the trees.

If Tangerine Dream (or Mogwai)
was in my head all day
that'd be just fine.

My brain cells are rebelling
like Keith Richard's lungs
from that, one last
Marlboro Red, screamin' bring it! Fuck death.

Everyone wants to live forever
and everyone deserves their own soundtrack, for the long ride.
For added sentimentality. I just want a coffee.
And a home to go home to.

If that home had a garden, that'd be neat.
I'd plant things nobody eats
like radishes, beets.

If I had a garden
I know stuff would grow
if I took care of it
and I'd take care of it, 'cause
soil's free. Water's free, right?

It falls from the sky
we no longer look up at
in big fat drops. And the sun
just sits up there and shines and shines
like the special kid in class with the thick glasses
musing out the open window, 'bout how good life is.

Eureka Springs

What can keep me from dreaming?

Days and my voice are both old.

All my clothes smell like moth balls.

My grandparents are dead, both sets.

The house I grew up in burned down
and the funny thing is
I'd just bought plane tickets
rented a car
and drove to the Ozarks
to show it to a girl
who now will never know it.

As a kid I had visions
of Jesus floating down the stairs—
having come from who knows where
with his airbrushed tan
and luxurious hair—
to stare at me while I slept.
Trying his best to read my mind.

The boy who lived here before me carved
HELP ME on the far wall of my deep, always-dark
even with the bulb-burning bedroom closet.
I went there for peace—
believe it or not—
and found it lurking
terrified of the light
that was thin and weak

just like me (empty tummy),
having spent my grass-cuttin' money
on candy and music magazines.

Feeling small beneath the closet's tall cedar walls.
Hiding behind shirts, jeans and coats
I never did grow into. Hoping
daddy wouldn't come home again, with his drunk, long-haired band friends.

In a big empty room
in a red-brick house that no longer exists
a little kid drifts off to Memphis Slim on his Walkman.
Dreams of dinner plates spilling over
with rice, beans, buttered rolls and meat.
A tall glass of homemade lemonade on the table.

Dreaming about eating instead of eating for real.

Relying on strangers for lessons.
Relying on charity for fortification.

The Emerald City

I want a tattoo of the Saqqara Bird
which means, I wanna fly away.

Anywhere away from here will do.

I wouldn't want to haunt this place
when I pass, and neither would you.
There's plenty hurt faces in church already.

Ghost Adventures came here once.
Filmed 5 episodes 'cause there was just so many
fine old homes, graves, caves and dives to explore.
Zak got EMF spikes while eating hot tamales at Solly's.

I don't want to die here.
Be buried so near the kin whose relations I tried escaping.
I wanna die in the neighborhood *Home Alone* was filmed in,
if that neighborhood was in Nashville, Tennessee,
(before the tornado) on the outskirts of the city.

Where a man can have and maintain land.
Surrounded by rich neighbors who eat turkey and candied yams for fun.
Whose kids attend the State University
and are constantly clad in the school's colors.
I could be their brother.

When I die, people like that might comb my hair.
They might put volumizing product in my thinning hair and comb it,
if I have any hair left when I go.
They may even let me borrow a nice shirt and tie
from the white garbage bag marked *for the poor*
sittin' outside their back door.

Those type folks have family, friends
who swing by for ball games, BBQs, weddings, graduations
and don't just stand around and cough, all tall and scrawny, like a Holocaust victim
drinking up all the beer, but who bring potato salad, without cigarette ashes in it.

Before I'm gone, I could ask people like them
to fake my worth. To praise me, build me up.
Make me almost one of them in the end. A volunteer *everything*.
Maybe so they can be forgiven for sins they committed,
if anyone's up there looking down on us, and cares.

Pray over my body, to Enki, Viracocha and Jesus.
Wrap me in a purple robe with gold frillies.
I wanna look like if I was still alive I'd feel like Elvis Presley, Marilyn Manson &
Judas Priest during their peak touring years.
As if I could and would snort up all the coke in the room
have sex with 3 groupies
then get out on stage
full of vigor! and become a god.

When my heart gives out
or I'm hit by a truck crossing Okeechobee
drape the sterling silver necklace your sister gave you,
from Mexico,
over me, even though you didn't know me.
I'm vain, in a way (we met at your mailbox that time)
and no matter how far I went I never got away.
You know what I'm saying
and I'm only saying it so you know I can laugh at my own jokes.

Ha! Ha! Ha!

Whatever you do don't be sad.
No, no.
Don't turn a good thing bad because you're mad.

Drink, listen to music, dance yourselves into hysteria.
Let go of the little control you have.
Treat the homeless to a coffin-side buffet at my wake.
Tell your neighbors a valet will be parking cars in front of their driveways.
What the hell, invite them as well.
Laugh and cuss and waste all the food your gardens ever grew
on my parting. Slay some deer too, yeah.
My feast needs meat.
Hunt them into extinction for me.

Giving is a gateway to redemption.

My conscience is a mighty wall discovered by the Inca.
Awareness of it (the reason it exists), is all there is.
Above it all. Keep everything out. Earthquake proof.
I know what happened on Mars.
I know who Earth was named after, and why.
He told me not to worry,
to purge all that worthless wishing (over blown-out, recycled birthday candles)
for visits from the old man.
Sometimes they leave for good.
Sometimes wishes come true.

Forget it. Change the subject: Isn't it tremendous
how dung beetles know
the Milky Way is there?
Not that they know it's the Milky Way, per se
or that it's there, necessarily
but they perceive its light,
and know how old and far away it is.

We don't belong here. No way we came from apes.
Some of us are allergic to bananas, the sun.
Animals don't kill for fun.
Hippos, maybe.
Bears and sharks, maybe.

We kill each other over parking spaces.
Shoot-up schools, malls, churches
'cause our little feelings get hurt.
We want to see what the insides of dogs look like.
Our best friend.
Mothers killing their children and selves to punish unfaithful husbands.
        We drive fast, eat crap, die young and dumb.

Maybe I'll get a tattoo
of some dude fighting lions—
two of them, on either side—
with GILGAMESH
written in Assyrian 'round the scene.
I'd be stylin' then. Even though life can suck he didn't want it to end early either.
One can always get laid.
Have an adventure. Get paid.

If I were *really* dead or dyin'
I wouldn't be talkin' so much.
I'd be as tight-lipped as the brothers
on the corner of 10th and Military, frontin' with the boombox.
Thinkin' though, has my head ringin'.

Good Eastern advice is so hard to consume.

If I were dead or dyin', guess who I'd wish I was?
Not some scumbag who had stuff

but a man, who knew something he knew was True.
'Stead of a dumb human
foraging through the refuse for clues,

who lived knowing nothing.

Rise and Shine

Masculinity
was seeing over the dashboard
of an old Jeep or Ford
that reeked of gasoline.

Who was I to interpret that moment?
The same speck of dust I am today.
The same Junkyard Kid from Oak Ridge.

Negativity clings to me
(like an NFL receiver's shrink-wrapped jersey
fits so tightly over his shoulder pads so defenders can't grab hold so easy)
though I shed like a 10 year old Labrador retriever.
My face feels like
if I was looking at myself
I'd be "Wimpy" Halstead's dead wife.

While walking through the woods
in Mississippi as a teen I seen
many thick-ass venomous snakes mistaken for Satan:
copperheads, cottonmouths, canebrakes.
The deadish, unblinking eyes, catlike, under squares of rusted tin
in the tall weeds, 'round the hunting camp cabin, waiting for prey.
Or sunnin' among the ivy engulfed lattice works of antebellum mansions
I worked at and got fired from—
some more than once—coiled up. Patiently waiting.

The old homes still stood like bold immigrants looking for work
among so many early patriots.

There were cannonball holes in the porches and roofs of most of 'em.
Owners patched 'em up with plexiglass but they're meant to be seen, I'm sayin'.

Tourists enjoy the thought of us suffering still.
It makes for a more rewarding, theme-style vacation.

I'm in south Florida now, that was back in the River City.
The Hill City.
Where the Civil War was lost.

Home of the Gators.
Home of the Vikings.
Home of those who ate rats and drank piss
to survive. To persist,
beyond the sins of their kin.

Water Fall

It was colorful that summer
in the hills of my mother's father.
The sun always set between two limbs.
Limbs I climbed on lonely days,
days when there was no ball to be played
or it was raining. Ate out the garden mainly
but every now and then we drank pops
and had ice creams from Brown's store up the street.

Behind the pump house
someone else's cows
chewed on corncobs and watermelon rinds
granny threw over the fence.
I feared the bull, his balls were big and his face was nasty.
He looked more pissed off than my grandpaw.
'Least I knew why grandpaw was pissed.
His teams always lost, so did he.
He was a Golden Gloves champ, long ago.
Had a sheet metal business in Ola, too
till one of the kids got sick and he sold it.

Granny shopped at Sears and JCPenney.
Bought clothes for me that were never in style
and way too big for my narrow frame.
They slipped off my shoulders
like a blessing from a firewater pastor.
Over the years she sent little gifts
that didn't have any significance
till I'd managed to misplace all of them.

In the low hills, north of Pleasant Grove
was a waterfall called Haw Creek.

We boys used to dare each other
to backflip off the tire swing
when it was up good and high
and dive into a pool of green so deep
I never could touch the bottom.
We'd spend a multitude
of summers carving I LOVE _____
in the sandstone outcropping
only to come back as bitter adults
and destroy it.

Foamy, cold water flowed
ferociously from the 40 ft high jagged ledge,
persistent as a hero pining for his dead friend.
Then one summer the creek dried up
and people from out of town figured
it made a perfect place
to dump and burn garbage.

We felt like Indians who had Spaniards with smallpox knock at the door.
Bearded, wearing shiny metal suits. The return of the gods.
Being too welcoming to strangers can backfire.
Our paradise had been discovered.
Our solitude stolen.

The crumbling schoolhouse, all us kids and our parents knew about
out in the witch's wood, near Marshall,
with the bloody handprints on classroom walls and in the halls
had haunted my dreams for centuries y'all.

But last night, some Yuengling drinking yankee trash
trying to make us look bad,

burned it to the ground
thinking it was a black church.

Burned it to the ground and brought hell down on a community of 12 dirt farmers who lost they crops and stopped believing in God.

Wives' Tale

Spin a good one
about how I'm never there.
See what happens.
See if someone cares, for long.

Cook up confectionery lies
about me like old witches
in old-growth forests
jealous of young brides. Hungry,
for healthy, panic-stricken prepubescent children.
All cackling, nude dancing
and spell sangin' 'round a bubblin' cauldron.
That's *you*. Your people. Jungle, ritual, superstition.
   I just enjoy watching boxing and drinking to dull the pain.
     The me who wants to keep his job and buy a home, sees you.
    But he only exists 8 hours a day. Jobs come and go.
Love is hook (if love is what it is)
and bait for babes
shook from the safety (the warm salty mac and cheese comfort) of pleasant dreams
too soon (prayed over, lied to)
midwinter nights,
in cities with names with too many syllables.
Too many full moons to have a break from the crazies.
That's me. Well, it's where I reside at least, so.
I belong in the country, I need to go.

I could never love that ugly face anyway.
That ugly face that ugly fucking patient privileged pretty indigenous face.
Not witchlike at all but classical, made-up
just and only for me, in this hateful city I need to leave.
Even if y'all won't come with me.

Worse than an alcoholic, country-singing truck driver.
Gone, already. Drink in hand, shifting gears.

I may be scared but I'll close my eyes
throw the covers over me
and you won't exist
won't have existed
ever existed
existed.

That's mist I see, out the window
taking shape.

Not the living memory of the girl
and legacy I let get away.

Smarty Pants

Can't reach the love inside.
Not for you, her or the baby.
I'm totally dead inside.
Want to commit suicide.
All because my computer won't work.
Then the printer wouldn't work.
I hardly sipped my champagne.
This is serious. Okay, okay.
I've said it, it doesn't get better.
It does but only for a minute.
I want a PhD in Divinities
from Barry, but I (can't believe in God)
committed to Bennington in fiction.

Okay, okay. That's so stupid.
What a dumb thing to say.
I thought M.P. might help me
arrange my book. He said it was brilliant.
Reminded him of Harry Crews.
This is all so lame, and he hated it.
What's in a credential anyway?
Will it help me pay the bills,
or give me another bill to pay?
Just spent half the rent on two new ink cartridges
an ounce of weed and three reams of paper too, dammit.

It's easy for good people
to get so riled up they forget
what's important and do something stupid
like shootin' up a church, mall or high school
(17 teens alone, just down the road from Boca Raton).
There is *no such thing* as a safe zone.

A loony walked into a burger joint
down the street from my house the other night.
Went on a shooting spree. Nigga reloaded three times
without anyone doin' shit. Some hid under tables, filmed it.
One dude died going back for the toy
missing from his kid's kids' meal. A fireman. A veteran.

I get the urge, the shakes, the sweats
but I couldn't hurt no one (yet).
Nope, they got babies and bills and junk
and like me, gotta go to a shitty job prob'ly.

I'd rather free fall with no parachute
off the world's tallest building.
Stretch my arms out wide and fly for a minute
before heading to the next dimension.

T W O :

blandscape

Fingers Crossed

I wait for her nevershowingupness
in the dripping, humid shade
of my grandpa's wood shed
listening to life inside the walls
all around me.

Wasps, with their legs crossed
hover in the uppermost angles
of gables like ghosts
with terrible news
they can't wait to deliver.

Waiting for a girl is like getting dressed for church
and dreading it knowing your grandmother will embarrass you
by speaking in tongues.

While exploring the rustic structure
I find my uncle's footlocker
from when he was in the Navy (model cars, porno pics, *letters*, pistol).
My grandpa hides his hooch here too.
It's covered in dust like a genie's lamp.
After blowing it off (particles float in the seeped-in light bars like spirit orbs)
I steal a swig or three.

That fine muscadine wine
aged almost to vinegar
makes me so dizzy I believe
Jesus is everywhere, and loves me.

Red wasps, *bright* red,
the mean ones,
have made a home above my head.

That's why this place is safe.
They'll sting if you look at 'em wrong.
It's difficult even to think of sinful things or else they sting.
So I wait and whittle a little bit.
  Sharp knife, thick wrists,
soft stick: A shape emerges:
A boy waiting
in a shed full of relics,
rusty nails and tin to snag his shoulders and toes on then die of a hick disease.

It was pirates who sliced me (tetanus),
was a shark what bit me, my scars are anydamn thing I want them to be.
  Waiting, waiting, *waiting*
for a girl who never shows up ever but knows just what to say always.
Dizzy with the thought of Jesus loving us
and being everywhere at once, not judging us.

Mira Flores

I was stabbed on 45th Street
in West Palm Beach
but that wasn't what scared me.
It was the needles, machines without feelings
and the alcohol smell at the hospital
where gorgeous nurses with big tits
inspected my injury from all possible angles.

My chest hurt,
blood ran all down my new shirt.
But my dick worked fine and did flutter a few times
like Fred Sanford's failing heart, at the thought of this being it.
Might never see the Great Pyramid of Giza.
Might never. Ever, and it's been there since long before the 4th Dynasty.
The entire waiting room was staring at me and my blood
wondering why I wasn't troubled enough to plug it.
Their wounds were in a deeper place I reckon.

The nurses had seen it all before,
calm, but busy as ants with their arms full of towels,
gauze and shiny stainless steel items wrapped in plastic.
They smacked their gum, winked at each other and nodded.
One with pink lipstick and bangs pointed at me.
Told two huge men to roll me to the trauma unit.

Everyone gathered 'round the gurney
like a cargo cult 'round a box of dropped goodies.
The men tossed me on a narrow bed and left the room.
The pretty nurses stood over me, praying to baby Jesus.
I averted my eyes and noticed
they all wore white shoes.
Their scrubs were mostly blue but one wore maroon.

She was telling the others what to do.
They were all Latinas with nice teeth
and smelled like cocoa butter & hot milfy sex.

Some hummed and swayed
to bachata in their headphones
as they walked in, and away.
Their prideful strides showed
they know they come from a long line of wise Andean elders
who lived amongst their gods,
mined gold, made beer and built temples for them.
An ancient race of priest kings and queens
living in little houses made of reeds.

You never heard a medicine man
from Puma Punku speak have you?
They're quiet, when they're not talking
and one feels rude saying *huh, what*
with his face all scrunched up, like a clueless ultra-modern fuck.
It'll make you think like a big boy, about big boy things.

A smooth-skinned nurse
with light in her amber hair
smiled down at me and said:
"Even though it hurts now, and will for a while
everything will be alright, with time."

Oh how I wanted to be at home
in my room on Hope Valley Street
after having just quit my job—
watching YouTube videos
of black folks reacting to Lynard Skynard songs—
drinking beer, knowing endings are beginnings.

In Santo Domingo (Vicksburg and Havana),
you can sit at an old bar

outside under an old tree
and look across the buckling street
at the New World's first church.

A man in his thirties, will ask to shine your shoes
many, many times.

It will probably rain while you're there too.
The damp, turned-earth smell will remind you
of the place you grew up
and the hatred you harbored for it all those years, gone.

I didn't identify then, though,
while in Santo Domingo, with being white
and the Swiss girl I was with
no doubt
wished I was darker-skinned and spoke Spanish.

I was thinking more like Akka-dian.

It's old school, but yeah.
I'm old school too, and yeah

The future is in the past.

Fair Play

I've seen Frazier rock Ali 50 times or more. The champ kept his gloves down after a clinch just fractions of a second too long, which means once they were down, it was already too late. I felt sorry for him. He was a genius in the squared circle. A good looking man, charismatic.

I have 48-3-1 tattooed on my right wrist and everyone asks what for. I keep them guessing. Most people think it's in remembrance of some loved one's passing until they realize the numbers are too wacky to represent the date of such a mournful occasion.

It's Tommy Morrison's professional record. He blanked hundreds of journeymen with the same sort of terrifying left hook as Frazier. Harold Letterman said they were similar. They'd dip, come up with the legs to generate power, pop. It's exciting to see men fall in the ring, after giving their all, instead of on battlefields, or murdered in the streets without a choice. Only one person I know of died in the ring. Many died horrible deaths long after they retired. Like "Irish" Jerry Quarry. When he was inducted into the World Boxing Hall of Fame he shook so violently he couldn't sign autographs. His brother had to hold his hand and say, "A circle, remember, with a line through the bottom, like this."

When you're winning you're king, and every man wants to be king. I wish I had a stiff jab, to keep a fool at range. A good left hook to the temple, the liver. I'm beginning to understand the importance of compact punching and keeping my mouth shut. Chin down, but not on the chest. When Bentt knocked Tommy out I could tell Tommy was embarrassed *and* hurt. Bentt weren't no chump either. Remember when McCall caught Lennox Lewis on the jaw with a straight right? Knocked his ass smooth out. McCall cried in the ring once and refused to fight. It don't get no lower than that.

He won the rematch. Lewis, that is. When "Iron" Mike got routed by Douglas I was happy the underdog won. White guys are always the underdog. Even after Cooney crushed Norton in 54 seconds, no love. Bernard Hopkins said he'd never lose to a white man, then got knocked out the ring by a cracker carpenter in his final fight. Still, nada. The Klitschko bros, GGG, Tyson Fury ... nothing.

Foreman said he was the hardest puncher ever. *Cooney*, that is. Punchers like him punch themselves out. Which is what happened when Morrison fought Ray Mercer. Tommy was a surgeon for four rounds but Mercer had the tougher beard. Had that thing inside that wouldn't give up even if he did. That, comeback spirit, that better not be slept on.

I appreciate a good fight. When it's fair. I do push-ups, sit-ups, I run, sweat, jumprope and look at myself in the mirror hoping someone pushes me, and that we both have time to empty our hands and remove our shirts before the other dude lands a punch.

Long Distance Relationship

Holy shit: sometimes, never knowing
becomes the truth.
We can admit it and feel better.

Take the money and run and
for god's sake, don't be sad.
The end was always coming.

From far away I knew and enjoyed you.

My kind thrive when the chips are down.
Don't identify with being Pisces
as much as being lost feels right, now.
Grief is at home in my bones.

What does that really mean?
A constellation in the shape of a fish.
Is it where we come from,
or the aliens who made us?

And so what, I feel at home in water
and love people who wish I was dead.
It's romantic. I keep a cedar chest
in the attic, full of letters and photos
and it smells like the history of men building cities.

Whoa, there I go, delivering bad news
when I should be the epitome of positivity.

Light in your eyes—with its own orbit
and tremulous glory—tells *your* side of the story.
It's so heartwarming and historic
I'm reminded of Wilfred Brimley's

holiday *dia-be-tus* drives. Sitting by the fireplace
in his comfy, broke-in recliner and Woolrich vest.
So eager to bless the audience with good advice
that he forgets the name of the movie he's introducing.
Dia-be-tus, ha! What a cozy, domestic, funny sounding disease.
Like, if you don't have it, you're not American.

His fat round body and whiskered face
were funny. His chubby cheeks and purple nose
were funny. Whatever he was trying to communicate must have been hilarious.

In a grandpa *I'm afraid of becoming* sorta way.
In a bitter, *peepin' out the blinds, can't mind my own business* sorta way.

Going Home Sucks

Going home sucks.
Not just the small town you hail from
but your shitty apartment in south Florida.

My mom lives here now
amongst us, and the new baby.
She cooks and cleans and babysits
and still it isn't enough.

I want everyone gone.

Until they're gone. Even the dog
with his pampered ass.
He barks at everything,
He's lazy, has terrible gas.
He'll eat a chicken wing covered in maggots
then hack it up all over the living room rug.
The baby is too much trouble too
and the payoff too far away.
Still, we need someone who will take care of us
when we're too old to cut our own hair
or wipe our nasty asses anymore.

I need someone who will take care of me
just before I die. When I can no longer walk or drive.
I'll work hard, at certain times, to deserve it.
The world will see me trying
to cope, to get by and they'll say
hey, look at that old bastard gettin' it.

Oh, but now I've done it.
I meant, once the baby's past the hating me stage

and starts to listen
is when my job begins. Until then ...

I've gone and done it (shown my cards)
made *Dead Father* sounds
from deep inside my gut.
I let those feelings turn to words and come up
from deep inside my growling gut.

Lonely people live in cities. I live in one now.
Been trying to get out.
Cities are where lonely people live,
hid away, in air-conditioned isolation.
Sometimes the AC goes out.
The power too when the house is full of people.
A football game, holiday or birthday party maybe.

Last night at dinner, my girlfriend took her fork
stabbed my slab of meatloaf and stole it off my plate.
It had ketchup and hot sauce and melted cheese on it.
I wanted it. What tha, nobody likes what I like.
But cats have the killer instinct, after all, not dogs.

Holy fuck!
I've become James Dickey's hungry lyin' ass.
Worse,
that pock-faced-fucking Bukowski character.
I'll toss this hardy plate in the garbage
eat a candy bar and drink 5 sodas.
(Remember what I told ya?)

Lonely people live in cities, like rats
(eat drink and mill about like scavenging writers).

To have a baby and to no longer exist as an individual is a blessing.
And uncircumcised pricks look like grub worms

with turtleneck sweaters on
when changing poopy diapers
from on high, looming,
Dead Fatherish.
Dumbstruck, blankfaced. Catfisheyed.

The responsibility on the shoulders of sudden fathers.
Fathers who are not worthless.
Fathers who are forever boys trying to buck their own breeding,
who'd prefer riding their new Mongoose
with the mag wheels 'round town,
out to the Indian mounds and back, than work for a living.
But bred to be soldiers, carpenters, mechanics, farmers, we work.

I liked it when, on a Chappelle show skit,
Charlie Murphy said Rick James was "mad niggerish."
Shit was gangsta.
Keeping up the good fight is gangsta.

I heard that once,
the bit about the prick,
many, many years ago.

(*snicker*) And the image stuck with me.

Sad Little Man

If I'm happy now
what will tomorrow bring?
Will my eyes get all wonky
at new opportunities like
Thom Yorke's eyes get all wonky
during serious interviews
and him always being so damn cool still.

My dad would say he's "slick."
Smoky motherfucker with a nice
holiday beard, good for rubbing
cheeks with distant family with and then
them not wanting to get close ever again.

The wretched smell of cigarettes after a bath.
Fresh pressed plastic, the numbers on a football jersey,
crisp, new, for Christmas. Ah, my letterman jacket goddammit.
I want it back from the hussy I gave it to in high school.

Wonky like vacation hours: *WHAT! FOR REAL! FOR ME!*
Wonky at the prospect of new, wonderful things.
Things that feel like
They'd smell like
the inside of a new pair of basketball shoes.
Nike Air Assaults,
with the safari trim and block print.

Wonky like the fat, bright green laces
I traded the kid up the hill my Ozzy posters for.
His parents owned a B&B
with its own cemetery
north of the post office on Elizabeth Street.
Where gifts used to come for me.

From such places as Asia, Congo, Dominica.
Naw, and places where wonky eyes are okay
as long as you can sing the blues and brother
this honky can sing the blues.

You ever heard
hey, *yo*, you remember?
 Or run for office.
You can headline a blues festival in the Delta
or run for office with wonky eyes.
But you might not win.
Good wholesome folks will think you're, how do you say ... *shifty*.

Sherwood Forest Blvd

Driving down the road.
Dixie Hwy, actually.
Where all the hookers are.
Locals do in fact call them "Dixie chicks."
With their sort of in-shape asses
but also their sort of flabby
homeless crack-head asses.

At any minute, all my
bald tires might explode
causing me to jump the curb
and run one over.

Then, just 'cause I been drinking
I'd be the bad guy.

Can't help but notice too
beside and behind the hookers,
a multitude of phone poles
and concrete dividers to smack into
should I lose control of the vehicle.

I'm glad no one I love is here.
Maybe my luck is changing.

My cd player quit working today.
Maybe it already *has* changed.

My sunroof won't close either.
A sure sign of rain.

I have two dollars and some change
crumpled up

in a molting McDonald's receipt
for a couple fish sandwiches
and a Coke in the console.

I'll give it to the guy bumming at the next red light.
He can have the sandwiches and the Coke too.

Wow, I feel like the generous kid I was a million ancient summers ago.
I cried once when a retard couldn't unwrap his silverware.
But he was white so, I didn't just walk over there, and help him.

Maybe I'll just eat it. I'm gluttonous, got the munchies and
he probably wants something he can fold to hold on to.

Clutter

Pal, your mom's hoo-ha
is a gateway to the afterlife.

Every man has
or needs, someone to report to.

Bad music is as hard to define
as making everyone pay
is relative these days. So sure, Orgy is okay.
I got nothin' against death pop.
How could anyone ever take an angle away?
Man said he gonna take my angle away the other day.

What's an angel
and why does everybody
think they have one
sittin' on their shoulder, watchin' over 'em?

Day to day activities
are no longer intentional
and increasing in arrogance.
As if I alone know the future
and have already started prepping.

Getting into character is easy watch
black & whites of Hitler doing it before a speech.

My knuckles are pulp
from punching trees,
from punching holes in walls the size of pies.
From getting into character. It's easy, watch.

A clever man said:
"Never judge a book
and be weary of women(son)
alone in the woods. Especially if she happens to be holding a hatchet.
If she can saw logs boy you better haul ass."
How can we get rid of so much damn useless clutter in our godforsaken skulls.
Hey?
Pal, your mom's skin is soft and bluish *like a ghost*. She knows what comes next.
I bet her husband is jealous of the punks she fucked when she was younger.
Her temple abode, is in In-di-a. *Your perpetually pregnant mother.* Get it, *blue skin*?

One should always Fear women
naked in the woods, (son)women with tattoos of upside-
down blue elephants and men, men with more than two arms
who swear to know where a certain flower grows.

Never Say Die

He'd lived in the South most of his life. Worked in Dallas for 3 or 4 months back in the '90s, but. Knew a thing or two about blacks being from Mississippi, where the blues was started, so he's more soulful than most honkies. Ain't afraid to dance, can play the banjo, piano. When he was a boy he'd pick and moan with the best of the front porch dudes. Had'a old soul, as they say. His hair's falling out now and he gave up living by the beach to go back home, chop wood, shoot food.

She's a Southerner too, from Colombia, South America, who just moved here for work at the auto assembly plant. Speaks Spanish, and a language that's almost dead now. With a harsh, sexy accent she said it was beautiful, lush and dangerous as hell down there. He reckoned it must be. He'd heard of Escobar, the FARC, the square and park in old town Cartagena. Her people have lived there since Adam and Eve. They have a myth of a time before the moon was in the sky, she said, when Saturn was a sun. He had a Navajo taco once, at Wupatki National Monument, AZ. That was traveling in time enough for him and he didn't want to venture that far from home again. Not even in his head.

Out of the blue he said, food brings people together, don't it! 'Cause he smelled food cooking (or the memory of the smells of food being cooked by nice, familiar grandma types) and it got the glands in the back of his jaw to fizz and pop with the anticipation of tangy BBQ sauce, soft, fall off the bone meat, which was weird because they were standing under a ceiling fan at Dollar Tree with no kitchen in the building. Maybe it was coming off the girl he just met. She did have a *we just ate* look on her exquisite moonface, and a Warren Central Woodsmen football hoodie on, made of dense cotton, good for trapping campfire and smokehouse (fieldhouse) smells for long times. How old was she? Did she have a child, a man?

He mentioned her eyes looking like Inanna's from a print he'd seen once at a swap meet in Leland long ago. Kinda like Michael Jackson's, kinda like an Assyrian princess's. She tilted her head left, squinted her eyes, zoomed in on him: *Who?* Healthy, thick, straight black hair shifted from one side of her face to the other, in a single, unified, historic motion. At that moment, he shared her people's memory of the Deluge. She'd never heard the name Inanna, said it sounded Royal, and like someone not altogether bad.

Her mother was with her. Old like the Andes. Fatish, sturdy, stocky. Close to the ground, with a gas station Saints cap sitting sideways on her round head. Heavy jade earrings hung and swung from stretched lobes and brooches shaped like roosters and llamas were pinned all across her Sasson sweater. The girl said they were symbolic, after she saw him staring at them.

He came to, out of a daydream (had traveled in time without meaning to), reckoned they must be. Lots of things seem to mean something other than the thing seen. Why not, he thought. He had something symbolic in his pick-up truck. He understood. Well, *on* his truck, that is, his wench. It meant he could get out of the shit when it hit. Or stay put, if need be. He was just thinking, other day, about how oracles in Greece might have had walkie talkies left behind by ancient astronauts, to communicate with their hot human whores. Then after a while the batteries died and the whores never heard from their birdmen again.

She could understand his fondness for his Ford, though folks don't have trucks much where she's from in Colombia. They like their motorbikes, she said, or they hoof it. People walk around here too, he said, like vehicles don't exist and gas ain't easy to get. Walking out of necessity is different than walking for health or recreation. But none spend too much time 'round Crow Mountain or Booger Hollow, 'specially at night. Too spooky.

That's where the ghosts and bears and bigfoots are. Rugged, beautiful, spooky. Night fires (forest) started by child-hatin' witches, occasionally cleanse mostly innocent villages while the sleepers sleep. Tornadoes break up tongues and disperse peoples who never lived anywhere else. So they can't get together and build a stairway to heaven, or a rocketship to get them to a planet so they can live forever.

She said her people have a legend of a feathered serpent, who was scary but also loved and worshipped. He traveled vast distances bringing culture and astronomy to all the dummies he met along the way. She said the farther south you go, like to Lake Titicaca and junk, he becomes more humanlike, like, someone who was here to do a job, boss people around and be mean. He wore a mask—*the god—*

47

because the people wouldn't be able to handle how he looked without it. They'd be scared and want to run away and he couldn't have that because they were slaves and had to stay.

The man who'd lived in Greenville, Mississippi, for most of his life said, yep. He was hip to her story. His god was scary too, and far removed. Was a hoarder of gold and silver and souls and just jealous as all hell. His god had made up a fabulous lie about redemption and forgiveness, to increase membership, and disguised it as the Truth. Thinking about there being nothing was deflating so to change the subject he said, when pumas cry, out in the woods, they sound like women being raped and murdered. But just know, when you hear it, it's pumas crying, lord knows what for. So just ignore it.

Oh, and welcome home.

THREE:

gut check

Fill Yourself With Dreams

Too many old men
tell stories about what glory is.
What it was in their day.
The youngins, pretending to be content
are jealous little terrorists.
I know, I am among them.
Fury runs deep for no real reason.

II

Good advice is wasted on me.
Save it for the depraved who need it.

Today, survival ends
and recovery begins. You must know
what I've done for you.
What I've done to keep memory alive.
And why, when I pray, I say take the pain away
but not all of it, Sir, Mother Earth, I think I'd miss it.
Leave just enough to make me hurt when I want to.

III

My very position in the cosmos is under review.
I will never cease being
this thing thinking
about trivial matters that don't matter
today, or any day.
The past waits for us in the future.
The past is our future:
A smoldering dead nothingness, floating in the abyss of space
waiting for some benevolent gravity to pull us to safety
so we can start ... all over again.

IIII

If only we could be naive beautiful baby boys and girls slobbering on new toys forever.
If only we could be naive cute sweet baby boys and girls with no past or futures forever.

We used to have it made. As teenagers
who didn't have to pay bills, could talk shit
be forgiven and still have a place to live.

We used to love on our ladies
and never ever complain
about anything but waking up early.

Back then, making the team
and maybe just maybe being kissed
by the redhead we were once
so fond of, was *every*thing.

Oh and music: Music: jamboxes
up against the ear, loud overloud
runnin' runnin' outta batteries
MJ, Slick Rick and LL
draggin'.

IIIII

Remember when? If you can, when the future wasn't in the past but in our hands.
In our hands, at our command.

IIIIII

Daddy had a job
for a minute
which meant we had Christmas.
Fireworks, ham. Presents.
I wanted what I shouldn't have.
My bro wanted a bike
which he got

and I got
once it rusted
and he was embarrassed being seen on it.

I would've taken care of it.
Would've kept it inside
out of the weather. Would've dusted her off.
Kept her chain clean, air in the tires.

Give one's self that one damn stinking right.
The right to want what we know we don't deserve
because it might make us wanna go out
and find a way to deserve it.

IIIIIII

I'm not giving advice, in fact
I learned an awful lot
from the entire time wanting myself
to so intensely shut the fuck up.

Sports

Bones turn to the stuff of who gives a fuck.
Trophies melt on the shelf and remind us
how good we had it when we didn't pay rent.

Line drills, gut check, run the hill. Thick Gatorade spit = down set 42 hut! Hut!
Ankle tape the color of team's anthropomorphic mascot. Hurt shoulder. Gashes
in helmet paint, painted over stickers from touchdowns and tackles. Crossbones,
New schools, new homes. Search lights blasting Potter's field for soon the game
will begin. Under an ancient mountain range erected to spook shivering children
into good deeds . Indian name, hid away, with indian turquoise necklace in cedar
chest with arrowhead hanging. You're here. I know hit. I know hit. In Mississippi
we always live with some old white dude's ghost, or the ghosts of a thousand
tortured slaves.

Let's swap shoes The "ghost"   sees us get off the bus. Let's swap
parents. It follows us into the house. Watches us snack on fatty foods and dream
of being tall and black with nice white teeth. Whispers, something about a special
plan for *me*. Mr. All SEC. Its coffee breath, whiskers, familiar. Whispers that sound
like screaming at low volume. Wood chop sounds and girls singing Appalachian
songs that aren't for sale. Girls who ain't the prettiest and who'll grow up to marry
preachers' sons who'll inherit 10 acres and a tractor when they turn 12 hallelujah.

We dribbled out to music, once around the floor, with our outdated, flare-
bottomed warm-up pants and rhinestone adorned tops. We'd dribble around some
before we started makin' lay-ups. I'd get the goosebumps try to dunk and jam
all my fingers. Some prick, I never found out who, would yell "BRICK!" Ouchie, I
played anyway and it took months to heal. Cold unhealed hands holding the reins
of a bucking barrel being yanked about by six alcohol deprived redneck teenagers
with a single goal. In the crowd the toothless hapless benevolent crowd some
yelling my name. Yelling for me to do something good. In the crowd see her I
love standing, clapping bouncing clapping like oh, now she knows how. And for
me, number 33. Got blisters blooming on my palms from being white, wanting to

impress all the brothers and dunk so I practiced and practiced and gave it hell in the Vicksburg ghettos. Jumped-high shot-straight talked-shit elbowed and returned fire with men thrice my size. Blisters don't go away so fast, no, they blossom and pop and leave big fucking sores that make a poor person look poorer for wearing bandaids all the time. I spent hours on the Super Cat building my calves up but there was never enough food around to bulk up on. I wanted people to notice my calves. Say they looked like Shawn Kemp's. I'd flex 'em 'round girls and twist at just the right angle to where they looked like a sculpted Greek god's. I couldn't stop trying to dunk even after I hurt my back, twisted my ankles and chipped teeth. Hunched over, Mick Mars style, back muscles burning, knees weak. I trained and pushed and played anyway. Could hardly raise-up the next day, but the night before I scored 20 points had 14 boards & 6 assists. We were doing what we were best at. During pre-game we jogged out to the House of Pain, ONYX and Cypress Hill. We danced to Garth Brooks in our letterman jackets with sassy young ladies whose hair was crunchy from hairspray and hardwater and smelled like *fire*. Could taste a hearty meal in their full-lipped French kisses: potatoes, shallots, milk, fish.

Later, after the game and after the beers and whiskey and Cokes. After we sprayed our bodies with Brut and called it clean. The girls' parts, charged, sparked and shocked me when raising sweaters off in the dark. Brothers warned of getting too close. Warned there'd be hell to pay. I had lots of bloody noses. It was worth every filthy stinking minute of it.

CONJECTURE

All we know is rumor.
It's critical we be glued to the TV
and piss our sheets nightly. Every little boy
will be god, *will have been god* in his lifetime
and being King will have felt good enough
to fight to keep the crown. Sorry to the birds,
all the birds of north Arkansas I blasted with air rifles,
wiping out untold family trees.
The eggs they protected, with their tiny-boned bodies,
spoils of my romantic, fucking-costly,
drawn-out doomed war. A body count, nothing else.

Sorry, to the multitude of lizards who lost their heads
in my courtroom made of sticks.
Sorry, but sorry won't bring back the dead, will it?

Kids are cruel. Kids are cruel they say.
'Cause the ones that have it bad
don't know anything about a better day.
And *we*, we plotted and schemed to get things
we needed, but smiled sweetly
in the face of authority
and pretended to be innocent
while good kids took the blame, and the spanking.

Was a handful of us boys and girls without family.
We'd meet on weekends and after school.
One's mama died of cancer.
One's daddy was hit by a train.
One lived with his granny who was blind and ate
government cheese and drank powdered milk.

From our treehouse hideout we discovered each other,
inside and out, playing games like spin the bottle
and catch and kiss. Looking up at the stars thinking,
we knew, know, we *wish* we knew, what femininity is
instead of hearing from men what masculinity isn't.

Women grow up to be ambassadors.
Women are grown up when they're little.
Boys grow up to be bastards. Ruthless amnesiacs,
more snaggletoothed and snarling
than any starving beast (indoctrinated into the system).
We must grow up. The world goes 'round.
It didn't stop for Enoch or Noah
so we got no chance.

If I had my old Haro BMX back maybe then I'd feel like a man.
A man who can fight wars and work his fingers to the bone
paying off credit cards, student loans and buying a home.

I own a long-haired Chihuahua and cheap Schwinn 10-speed.
Its gears have always confused me, made me look stupid
to a group'a homos smoking outside a coffee shop
once and them making fun 'cause they thought
I was trying to come off macho.

When my father died he left a chrome .45
and a box of homemade hollow-points for me.
For moments of weakness, like this.
He must'a thought I'd fold
at the first sign of adversity, like he did.

Someone punch me in the teeth please.
Shake me from my lame duck fucking musings.

The past is the past and I'm all outta sad.

Family Affair

I can't understand your words
so why try. Nothing is accomplished.
Wanting space is vindictive
apparently, end of story.
Maybe I'll quit my job
and go bye-bye. Go back to what I know.
But I can't leave my baby boy behind, and
can't raise him alone.

Knowing myself as frequency and light
shocks and maims mainstream academia.
Because I know about Sumeria,
matriarchal Egypt and Sophia.
Hey, it's your voice against mine.
And I'm just a liar, so *you* say.
One who knows we don't come from primates,
that men are not the same as mothers
and that mothers' voices are not deep enough,
bold enough, to scare a boy straight.

The idea, of a poor child doing anything significant in life
crumbles, like the tallest mountains into oceans of sand
that used to be giants' bones, and all over again.
Our memory of the incident lies fossilized
deep in our pineal glands, a dream within a dream.
Neither can a mother teach a boy to play football, or fight.

I was gonna be like Jason Lee
(the pro skateboarder, not the actor),
then she asked me to dance at Homecoming and the rest is history.
She's been in every room I've been in since
and I can't seem to shake her,

or the lingering smell of what it feels like to remember
when I gave up on myself.
Brut, Actif Blue, maybe. Old Spice. Wings.

Is needing space so bad?
I'm saying!
Is wanting to be an individual so cruel
that you need to remind me what you'll do
if I go away for a while. Maybe I'll rent a room on the beach,
Hollywood Beach, write jokes for TV. Listen to BB and Albert King
all by myself, 60 ft from white sand and green-blue sea.
Is wanting to drink, be alone and think such a terrible thing?
I'm not calling for a comet or asteroid
to destroy the Earth again, no.
I could be strolling the boardwalk, in my pink Golden Girls tee,
happily, and tan, wide brimmed sun hat (UPF 50),
the one that always makes me feel touristy though we're here 15 years now,
looking for a bar that'll serve me so early.

My damming up,
like Arizona did for tourism dollars
is a deep, cavernous warning
about the way things ought not to be.
So I won't go there, to Glen Canyon
'cause that's not right.
Pretty though, and the water's deep,
clean from what I seen in pictures.
Spent time in Prescott,
and the wrinkle-faced Natives
drinking hard liquor in the square
made me feel like I'd been born in a bottle
and didn't belong to this world at all.

But created, conditioned. Reconditioned.
Long ago a doctor noted that my skull was thin,
as if I'd been in zero gravity or somethin'.

We can't go home, too far away.
Not our childhood home in the hills near a clear river either.
Our cosmic home, in the stars, Lyra.
'Cause like dummies we still use fossil fuels.
Have severed ties to the Great Spirit (We Are All Indigenous).
But we can go somewhere else
and try to make *that* place home.

You in one hemisphere, myself in the other.
We'll destroy it over time as we spread, settle and (re)create.
We'll destroy it together, as we celebrate having made it.
Then I'll need you to go away again,
so, we may have to get inventive.

If you go away I'll want you more. As you know.
May even   miss you.

Or, we can stand here and fight about it
till the end of time

as brother and sister might
over the last slice of pumpkin pie.

Dummy

Dreaming about her has brought it all back
and she's pretty as ever. The sexy
scar above her upper lip, from fighting
was a constant reminder to be kind to her.
The year 'round aroma of her pits,
sweet like after-sex panties,
made my tongue wanna do tricks down my throat.

Ringlets, dark as Gypsy eyes
fell to just above her boney shoulders,
the most honest thing I'd ever seen.

Could speak foreign languages
with her big wet mouth, never nice
and always loud. I was proud to have her,
when she made me believe she was mine.

Folks saw us holding hands,
and for a minute, I wasn't just a snaggletooth poor-as-shit kid
with course red hair
who wasn't ever going anywhere.

Her father was a priest and hated me.
Her brothers Les and Chester too, were jealous of me.
They miss seeing that naked tornado
raisin' hell around the house.
They must miss, so much, being able to
catch and hold her back.

Her pasty pimpled face,
pretty but not pretty,
held two forest green pools

what looked like moons
controlling the tides and giving life.
Her long legs, peach-fuzzy and bruised
were summer in a jar forever.

We skipped school by the creek
with our warm sodas and sack lunches.
We kissed, played games and fished with crickets.

She's not dead or anything either, just
moved to Texas to get away from us.
Fell for a dirty dude who
drives a tour bus for Cake.
   She was a slut anyway, and hey, who can blame him?

Playin' the Fiddle

I am *not* (just) a riddle!

You are a window in my front door made of oak.

No one walks with me,
nor are we or anybody else archeo-
astronomers, paying attention to the stars, but
a gaggle of rat-faced cracker farmers with grudges against the government.

Shine a light on me. Please. Guide my dumbass home.
Salvation is the hardness
of things that won't decompose.

When we think, we travel in time.
Can't think of a time when we don't think,
but we can never go back to the beginning.

Tell me something.
What god's lies do you believe?

Have you ever heard of Enki? Who are we?
Behind the pulpit: **Rat faced cracker-bastards**
almost as bad as Portuguese and Spaniards.

I'm no historian, back from the dead. No Herodotus but
in exchange for the truth, willingly accept donations of cash, drink and food.
I'll accept, yes, in lieu of friendship, a job. PHD? Some PHD!
Let me alone. I have a teaching certificate and poetry degree.

There's a window in my front door [   ].
Sometimes I stare out the open window of that closed Oak door.
There's an airplane writing positive messages in the clouds.

I need a Spirit Box (SB11) to reach you now. A Mel Meter maybe.
(The positive messages hurt more than the real thing.)
Your cinnamony breath was so-like opening Christmas presents
and whiffing the newness of the thing within. But that was then,
before you jumped off the Yazoo River bridge.

What you *did* do by doing it is reignite my hearty appetite.
I accept this donation. A seed is worth a lot to me.
Cash and food would be good too. Kinda, down on my luck.

You are telling me something, that transcends time and space
and that's great, except, I'm too ape-like to concentrate
on anything besides munching ripe delicious bananas, mangos.

Proper Burial

The parts of me that matter most
are made of metal.

Walter Butts said,
"Anyone can be original."
Then he died.

In his day
happiness was a myth
a soothing story
old folks told kids

who had stories of their own to tell.

Well, metal rusts, you know.

As do dreams of living forever
in treehouses, in forests
and keeping the one true thing.

Okay, I lied,
and so what if I do.
Who among you deserves the truth?

Youth, is a myth.
We're always old,
sour-faced and irritated.
Dumb as a two-day dead tuna
and just plugging on away like the slaves we are.

So *what-if* I never told a lie?

Would you melt down sacred objects
to mold and shape
a mask made of gold for my stupid face?

When I die
will you take the time
to find my lucky Chucks
and bury me properly

beneath a magnolia
in south Mississippi?

Full Time Daddies
(interlude)

My puppy wonders where he came from.

He gives me horse-eye and lets me know
he knows, I'm not his daddy.

And for some reason this hurts me.

I ask if he wants a treat
but he just turns his head and snorts.

He's over it, apparently, and me.

To hell with him then,
and his gravy friggin' train.

We'll see how much he likes
working for a living.

I'm kidding.

He's just a puppy.
He doesn't have thumbs.

Not that can twist knobs
hold a hammer
or write letters back home 'bout
how everything is just great.

'Bout how much he
loves the city and everybody in it.
How he's eating right

taking all his vitamins
has lots of friends
and not drinking too much.
So, don't worry anymore, okay.

But puppies don't have mothers they report to
who always need to hear good news, do they.

No, puppies mommies & daddies go away, and for good
at an early age. Sad.
Mine live less than an hour away from where I stay
and still I can't find a way to say anything to make their days   better.

Moment of Impact

Smoke
Against the wall
After blowing the candle out
Looks like a ghost
From where I'm sitting
On the couch
With a bottle of whiskey
Listening
To my new favorite album

Deddy

Mean money maker, mad and hurt 'cause his role changed dramatically over the course of so many brutal wars. But he don't know this. Rendered now to that of a mere commodities provider and awkward affectionate. His kind has gone from soldier to babysitter to bank teller often enough to confuse any notion of becoming better mothers. They don't always know how to be daddies. Neither will we. Tendencies linger indefinitely, homeboy. That, and awful cock-rotting diseases, is why I carry condoms.

FOUR:

over the mountain

Climate Change

We don't need
algorithms
    to love, alright.

We don't even have to love
we can just get along, be partners.
        What if that was enough
    and we didn't have to worry about
losing it all after it took so long to get, what little it is.
What if we never had to worry about tornadoes or hurricanes, or being on time
for a job we despise? What if we could leave this place right now and ride out?
Wouldn't that be nice. No more ice storms, droughts or beach lice.
They say we're different from computers 'cause
computers don't know about themselves. But what good is awareness
when we can't remember we have amnesia?

    I hate my human heart.
    It's smarter than lots of computers are

    and has more space for storing painful things.

Grown Up

I knew I was old when I got
all huffy 'cause I couldn't find
a Barry Hannah book in hardback.

I just had to have it.

I immediately ran to the bathroom
to have a look in the mirror to see
if it was indeed true, that I was
an old crusty bastard.

Maybe I'm grown up
Maybe not, I wanted that hardback boy. The new shit.
Just before or after he died shit.
I'd hoped to find a first edition.

I collect things.
Collect books,
photographs of old porcelain skinned white women
I pretend are my distant kin.

I collect stuff. Letters, cds even
even though they're obsolete
now and we feel (and look) foolish
fumbling to get one out of its
case and into the player.
My gosh: Metallica, Nas, Slayer.

I'll be forty-three in March,
and more of a Counting Crows type-fella now than I was before.

All my sports injuries hurt. From back when.
I was invincible then, for real.

My body and mind were tested
on a daily basis.
It's winter always now, in my Christian Laettnerness.

I still have all the baseball cards I had
when I was a kid thinking
the American Dream was a possibility.
I loved Michael Jackson, back then
(his music, that is, not the child molester),
Lenny Dykstra and the Fresh Prince.
Had a pair of British Knights hightops and a red leather jacket
with a dozen bright silver zippers.

Back then, it didn't matter what you looked like dancin'
long as you were movin'. A wave of black and white
packed tight, in a dark, smoke-filled Jackson juke joint.
Weren't really any Mexicans in Mississippi then.

Back then, we could wear colors
we didn't have to die for.
We skateboarded, wore baggy jeans and shorts.
No neighborhood was off limits.
I could wear a gold chain, let it swing
till it knocked out all my teeth
and none of it, in any way
reflected a platform or system of belief.
We were free. Only a few ever accused me (Public Enemy, *It Takes a Nation of ...*)
of wanting to be black,
though Southern honkies cut our teeth on R&B, soul and rap.

On the football field, where a kid could be a god,
bold colors struggled for control of the pigskin.
The glorious purple and white of Saint Al's Knights.
The mean kelly green of Culkin's Crusaders.
Off Washington Street, near the haunted hospital
that was once a home.

The one with all the cannonball holes
and busted out windows. All overgrown with kudzu now
moldy and falling apart, is where our games were played.

My voice sounds like old bones
getting up to answer a ringing phone.
My breath must smell like musty mismatched
cleats in the corner of the boys locker room.

I'd hoped to come across
as a pleasant fellow, who knows
a city and her people. All her colorful people
living and working in the Haunted City.
The city that floods and fights and fucks.

I'd hoped to come across as a pleasant fellow.
Really, have I done it?
Are you convinced

enough to come for a visit?

Superstition

The CLOCK face men
have set their watches
to half-mast 10.

I wonder whose funeral it is.

See flags and rifles and medals.
There must be fifty cars in line
all shined-up and horn-tootin'.

At the end
there's a long Lincoln limousine
muscling its way through the gathered yokels.
In back of it
in an all black outfit
sits a horny-lookin' housewife
with her head hangin' low.
Her dark scarf flappin' out the window
as if in declaration of surrender.

It'd probably be white then, I suppose.

Grab a button
before the procession passes us,
or we may very well be next
and no one wants that.

Except maybe our dads
whose dicks are in the dust
and whose bright futures turned to rust because of us.

Mine always says he had it made
but that now he's just, had it.
It's kinda funny him throwing punches at the sun

like some infallible dude up there
is watching, knows
and really gives a shit about this planet and our woes.

We Was Kids

We was just kids
but wanted to be men.
Wearing our fathers'
and older brothers' wool
warish-pukish-greenish winter coats
with always gold and no other color buttons.

Some had more patches and merits than others.
A point of pride for kids whose dads died.
Some had real pistols, some had sticks
and we pretended to kill and imprison.
Mostly though, my conflicts took place inside the temple.
So, I have no bread to give you
or anyone else. No answers,
no Tablet of Destiny to gift you with then Indian give.

I used to be young and afraid
and stupid enough to care.
Since then I seen and done
things that'd rot an early pumpkin.

Youth, if ever there was such a thing,
was the skating rink
I busted my head on the floor of
so many times. Shit, I'm half stupid
'cause of-it. I know.

You don't owe me.
No one ever did.
Apologies are meaningless.

I'd love to owe *you* though,
if it meant you coming 'round to collect. (You hadn't been mentioned yet, but in you come)

78

Except my fortune is all spiritual. I,
there, there was and used to be an *I*.
At one time. Before the accident.

He was a dreamy piece of shit too, that loser.

If I had 3 wishes, *shoot*. I wouldn't wish
for the winning Powerball ticket.
I'd wish for a time machine more than anything.
So I could go back and save the animal
that was once my dear (older)
dead, fucking, decomposing brother for my mother.

Fairhope

County truck
half sunk

in storm water
and clay

makes its way
to the fallen tree

blocking the road
to my home.

In the rusty rising river
I *am* Ziusudra
the half-human son of Enki.

But he didn't bother to warn me
about an impending calamity,

or supply me with a plan
on how to build a boat
and navigate it to safety.

No, he has simply let me alone.

Maybe I'll burn some sage,
say a prayer, a spell
for good tidings and change
next time I visit my brother's grave.

Beyond the Grave

When fire is at our fingertips
we congratulate ourselves
immensely. We're men.

Our picnic baskets are packed full'a bullshit.
No wine, olives or fresh fruit. Ants
will carry the sliced meat away in time, you'll see.
We're from Tennessee, not Greece.

When the sun gets close
my soul vibrates (warm) with warm
colors from beyond the grave. Feeling as if a place called home exists.
Feeling a frequency no one I know can fathom.

Unimpressed, you see me
below the average
time of my longest line of credit.
Which reflects poorly on me, obviously.

Fish fries,
for families without food,
smelled and tasted like
baby lies, that hurt to keep inside.
Still, we did it. Though the adult us wishes we didn't.

Hot toddies for the child—
already sick with the numbness of routine—
will ease his busy mind. Calm his tummy. But he'll never (they Lord God!)
amount to much anyway, you'll see.

So let him sleep
among the vibrating, groaning sun
and gathered stones in this old, spooky hollow.

81

It's well known, after all
dreaminess doesn't always turn
kids into idiot adult asshole scumbags.
Kids see eye to eye.
You got it.
I want it. But in a nice way.
Let's make a trade or I'll take it.
Okay. OK. And in a nice way,
let's trade families.
You can have my about-to-die uncle who lives with us (and coughs alot) and my new
Luke Skywalker for your Father, his steady job
and your Han Solo, lil' bro.

The People's Champ

She's in my favorite spot.
Young gal, short shorts, sweaty-hot.
Can see her blossoming body from the parking lot
of the junkyard across the street,
swingin' on the front porch, daydreaming
of being a famous actress with a mansion in Dallas.

Everyone wants to become something we're told we can't or shouldn't be.
I'm going to be a WBC champion and fight on TV
before millions of fans who adore me.

Her home has more angles than a town hall whore.
Bet it's got more ghosts than St. Louis Cemetery #2.
Every boy in the neighborhood wants to cut her grass—
to catch a glimpse of her ass in pajamas thru a window—
which has driven prices down well below the normal rate.

I want her. Her skin always smells like white soap that floats.
Will shoot myself in the heart for her, 3 times,
like what's-his-name in Arkansas,
then call the law from the lawn where I lay. Hey,
what do you know about dedication?

This is fucked up. Royally, what a pain
to be ugly and horny in the 10th grade
with no one around to say it gets worse with age.

Seasons change, but I don't.
Leaves go from red to yellow to dead
on the ground all around the Dodge
that never run no-way but was the object
of lots of lies between fathers and sons. Daddy

don't celebrate Halloween either. He fixes cars. Plays guitar.
Halloween is for pagans, he harps, from his favorite seat at the bar.

We're all every one of us pagans and the changing leaves and decorations
on Water Street are pretty.
Symbolic of a new beginning for the world around me.

No one has proof I'm here. I'll disappear. Just tell me to.
I'll do it, if only you'll notice me when I'm gone.
Slip syrupy love letters in my locker and weep.
Don't lie to me. Tell the truth or I'll slug you and leave.
But I'll return. I want to be your first.
I'll save up, get a new carburetor and radiator for the truck.
I'll pick you up, late at night, on a school night.
We'll fill her tank up, head north on 95.

Talk about our lives and listen to the Hives.

She looks mighty clean to be so old, the Dodge that is.
It *don't* run though, and when it did it sputtered, smoked.
Daddy said it's better off being a home for bugs.

The inside smells like gasoline.
The vinyl dash and seats cracked and ruined.
There are wasps inside wanting to sting me over nothing.
Then grandpa will put tobacco juice on it
and say, *Stay away from the junkyard young man!*
The Original People person in him
will rub turmeric and cayenne and tobacco juice on my wound.
It'll heal quicker, he'll say, under his breath
as he turns for the busted-up screen door
to the back porch, back to the garden and the flies.

I wasn't hoping for a miracle.
Maybe a little miracle, and I don't wish
for a reason to get close to grandpa's stiff whiskers ever again.
Though he's a cool Injun from Omaha.

I come from, but am no simple farmer, swatting flies, drinking cold coffee.

If only she knew who I'd grow into, like *I* do,
her cousins and brothers and mother might approve.

We could meet under the bleachers, get high and drink the peach moonshine
my homie Brian hides at my house. We could eat burgers and fries from Pirate's Cove.
I got no money though, no credit card to charge somethin' on.
Poverty's a state of mind, folks say, and all suffering is thought based.
Okay, I'll shake it off. I'll stop thinkin' 'bout all that stuff.
She's not hungry anyway, they have meals where she lives.
As a family, 'round the square table, under the always lit chandelier from Ireland.

We have a 3 legged something or other no one ever sits at.
Even with the Monroe phone book under it it still wobbles and will spill your tea quickly.
Got a fridge full of stale air, half-drunk bottles of beer and a piece of weird looking meat
too small to sufficiently feed a boney, starving teen.

Don't be angry, let go. It's all "thought based." Get born again.
(Psychic flexing, lots and lots of internal huffing and puffing
'cause that's what a man is now)
Boxers don't need words, good looks or fancy cars.
They have fists. I'm the kid who intends to whip Mike Tyson with mine
worse than Buster Douglas did. I can handle it,
and much more. So bring it.

Going the Distance

Sometimes
in the middle of the night
if I wake up and it's quiet
I'll pray that something bad happens.

So we have to learn to depend on one another again
instead'a being so goddamn fucking selfish.
As if we're fending off intruders
always, from the lush, giving vines
of our post-apocalyptic Gardens.

We pray
like insects
for opportunities to be better people.
To planets, to Mother Earth,
we pray, to a plethora of Gods, ancient and modern
to be better people.
To be worthy of blessings.

And when we get what we want,
we go back to acting the exact same way.
Driving like assholes, cuttin' in line and
buyin' up all the water, hand sanitizer and gas we can find.
There's not one roll of TP in all of West Palm Beach.

Ah fuck it.
Destroy us.
Bring on the earthquakes, mudslides, tsunamis.
We don't deserve shit.

We'll just ruin it.

Pun'kin

Sometimes,
Smashing someone's face in
Sounds so cool
I wanna do it.
Like it's the right thing.
People are stupid. Mean.
Been watching the scary news on YouTube.
Like city animals
They eat trash, believe lies, fight.
Believe lies because
It makes them feel good.
As if it was ever
About them (takes the place of a lost thing)
Feelin' good
In the first damn place.
I am one, seriously.
I tell you. Shitty with wanting revenge.
Wasted life.
Drugs, alcohol.
Liver upset.
Topsy turvy feelings.
Hot fucking dirty sun.
Racial upheaval.
Being from Mississippi.
Media hounding.
White boy entourage.
Rebel flag wavin'
Bushwick Bill rappin'
Dead brother havin'
Lone-ass little nigga.
Birfdays
Hand-me-downs.

Dead cops.
Sirens.
Riots.
Square one.

Been dreamin'
Dad's driving us
Way too fast up Scenic 7.
My girl and baby in the back seat.
My nose is bleeding.
My teeth are loose.

I woke up. No one was there.
The sun-lit room broke into morning,
punctuating the moment, like a rib thru the heart.

The Daily News

The moment of impact
is not instantaneous.

Nor is it peaceful,
but the opposite.

Often the end
is so much
like the beginning.

FIVE:

a spark, at last

Canyon Country

If I had a pick
or a shovel
I'd dig a hole in the earth
until it was deep enough
until it was bottomless
then I'd leap off into it
like an old-timey stuntman
falling from a saloon roof,
making faces & clutching my
heart as I fell. Slow motion.

That'd be rich, cinematic.
Bystanders would whistle & clap.

Except there'd be no
cameras & it'd be too dark
to see me, not being afraid
but proud.

Proud of going out
like I wanted to
& not with my heart exploding

or my prostate & colon swollen.

TORN

between
being a man
and being
polite.

If I said
anything at all
I'd probably say

I'm not a calculator, okay.

To live easy and free, as you do
is not like being a hunter gatherer.
It's like not having to hunt or gather at all and still have a tall glass of buttermilk,
fried eggs, bacon and bread
on the table every morning
without worrying about
who made it, laid it out.

You'll complain too
(with angry eyes and lusty lips)
'bout how loud my music is
and how the entire house smells like shit now.

I don't mind it. Not one bit.
I enjoy watching you smoke your morning cig,
all angles, at the open window facing the street. Daydreaming, about endless
summers, jobless endless sunny rainless summers, and your Latin lover, on a train
in Spain, looking out the window
feeling the same way.

Coming Home

I'll take care of you.
Can tell you need someone to
who's willing and able.

There's too many people at the park today.
Their happy times is killing my buzz
kids running through the cricket sounds and hot grass
clickin' and poppin' girls hoppin' broke fences
to catch up with freckle-face boys with cane poles slung over their shoulders.

I'll forget you when you need me to.
And I'll continue to send mixed signals only the teen in you can appreciate.

My dreams roller-skate backwards, 'round the rink (Big Wheelie).
Ask you to dance and maybe you say yeah.
Wanted to take you to Long Pool, the rope swing (the house)
but it was cut down decades earlier. Took you to the rock though,
'least you could see how we ran down its elongated face
launching our young bodies into the cool green pool.

I'll have a good job one day,
if you hang on a bit you'll see.
I'm studying important stuff
don't give up on me.
I read *Crime and Punishment* finally!

I think I get it. It's about Redemption, isn't it?
Well, I only strived for perfection in sports. Sorry,
and my lies didn't scare you away like I hoped they eventually would.
Your Indian hair was what I always wished for,
wanted my kid to be born with.

Going somewhere, hand an airplane.
Outside the window
a no man's land. Outside the passenger window
of Bobby's busted-up Mazda my hand was a Falcon 2000.
Head resting near angled elbow.
Going somewhere
(gone) out west, New Mexico, yes.
Reservations, ruins, checkpoints.

Coming home, I was coming home.
Then, 'cause then I lived with you
in New Mexico, with all the snow
and different colored deserts.

I was coming home, to the never warm water
of living on high, and still might. So don't go sell my drumset yet, alright.

Fall in a Small Town

Apples are round

and shiny and red and crisp.

Some are green and yellow and slick.

Some are red and green and small.
All are good and round and crisp.

Many rot and fall to the ground and stink
like moldy athletic socks
left in the locker room
without being washed
for an entire Miss'ippi summer.

Like coming home
to a dead pet or relative
after being gone on the Natchez
Trace for several days camping with some weirdo who knows nothing of being
a man 'cause ain't no man ever around 'cause they got families to care for and
can't get away to go camping with kids without fathers to teach 'em who a father
is, what a father does. Slim here's got a Fuck Trump shirt on though and he's
bangin' away on his lame ass bongos, talkin' 'bout some Yaris-driving silly hate-
America shit that no one gets and he just looks stupid. He probably doesn't have
a brother, sister or even a friend he can test his theories out on so he just throws
himself into the conversational fire.
Like people who don't know history. And not just what comes from books.

Ideas are like apples.
The good ones can be baked in pies and Danishes and given away
as gifts that keep giving.
Some are okay.

Most just kinda sit there
spoiling like unfinished holiday dinners
till they turn to liquid and drip, drip, drip
off the dining table and on to the hardwood floor.

I mean, everything we think we know is bullshit.

Then the flies.

The flies and gnats
tell the truth by god.

They'll get to you, regardless of the deterrent you use.

Matthew

It was so fucking hot.
Humid, as tourists like to say.
As if all my life I'd never really had a life at all
But had always been on set
For some civil rights movie filmed in Port Gibson, Mississippi.
Or out near Eagle Lake, Farte Cove and so on.
Where God still punishes good people, in the form of a Flood
To see if they will still be good and teach their kids to be good
Even though no good ever comes to them except when
Their crops are allowed to grow, be harvested and sold.
(Pssst. It's not God that created the Flood, it's the Army
Corps of Engineers. They flood the land, make it unusable then swoop in and buy cheap.)
All the little helpless animals running for higher ground and there is none.
Why the hell do you think ancient peoples built mounds.
So they could damn well see from elevation.

Some time had passed since last I wanted
To think and drink, listen to music, watch boxing and cook.
Put some Peach Pit on and chill, but a hurricane came.
Last night, we knew for weeks it was coming.
When it finally came thru we all wished
It had done more damage than what he did.
Yeah "he," his name doesn't matter.
It wasn't chosen of any heroic notion.
Baal didn't cause it,
Just ... following suit.
I have a baby to protect.
For me the storm meant more.
I wanted it to destroy. Wanted howling winds, the speed of which
This planet has never seen.
We taped all the windows with duct tape and heavy blankets:)
We didn't have storm shutters or tools or plywood.

We huddled, said all the prayers
But wanted it to destroy the neighborhood.
Cut down all the strip malls, vape shops, car lots.

Said lots of prayers and included people I haven't prayed for
In a long time so God would know I was sorry, and humble.
Everyone prayed and prepared and bit their nails but wanted to see destruction.
Something the news would rather fake
Than really show. Notice they never show
Any of the bodies or blood and gore from
Mass shootings? (useless clutter) Las Vegas, 59 fucking deaths: no bodies.
Not one blood-soaked sheet-covered image of a victim.
Parkland, Sutherland Springs: nothing.
Just pics of cops standing around smoking cigarettes
Directing traffic, and yellow tape. Lots of yellow tape.
A convoy of fire trucks and ambulances parked
Too far away from the scene of the alleged crime
For not one of them to be seen pushing a gurney at least.
No blood or gore or bodies anymore.
We believe without proof, 'cause who in the world would want to ...

Well, after wishing it, it began to rain hard
Till about 10 o'clock. Then I fell asleep.
Had dreams of loose teeth and going to class naked without my homework.
The baby fell asleep. Later in life he said he'd
Had dreams of Mason jars with faces speaking to him from under brackish water.
The house got darker.
We lit candles. Found flashlights with batteries about to die.
The wind rolled in like an old friend
Congratulatin' and pattin' me on the back
After such a long absence.
It felt almost great.
Like time machines exist.
I wondered where my dead brother is.
If there's a way to reach him, others.

The palm trees were bending and swaying.
All manner of trash was being thrashed about.
Car alarms, home alarms,
Abandoned animals, shopping carts, palm fronds.
Rebellious people walking/standing slanted
In the wind and rain and noise and debris.
Their face flesh messed up,
Undulating, gyrating
Like an astronaut's in a grainy NASA moon mission video.

The house creaked, it moaned,
It stretched and yearned for a life of its own (Anchuca, Cedar Grove).
Windows busted, trash and leaves and sand blew in.
My degrees and boxing photos blown off the wall and smashed.
My grandma's ashes lost in the blast.
Goodbye grandma, this is better than dumping you in the river
Or on some heavily trekked mountaintop near Denver.
Goodbye grandma,
I love you as much as my son loves my mom.

Across the pond, before it hit, folks
Boarding up their windows, drinking
And hammering and laughing, seemed to be celebrating
Their ignorant defiance too.
Like ourselves, but more outwardly.
Because we're just so damned tired of running I suppose
And want and need so badly to not be
Afraid of anyone or anything anymore.

Defy the government. Fuck 'em!
Fuck all candidates for all posts.
Do not believe (they want to change the system but the system changes them).
Do not vote.
Do not follow.
Do not mortgage your life away.
College is for suckers. Unless someone's life depends on your acumen.

Even if we die and come back here, life is great.
(Heaven isn't real, come on, streets of gold, all our dead relatives in one place.)
This time we'll come together, like we're One race.
Like before the nuclear incident that changed our skin color.
We'll build community gardens where prisons once were.
I'd have another chance to make State with the Vicksburg Gators.
I wouldn't blow it this time, with Lucia, or Kate.
I'd tell my mom I was sorry for calling her a quitter
When she left my father the dreamer, the renter.
If I could go back
I'd be better to the bloodhound I bought
To take the place of all the hate
I lost when I wasn't mad about my brother Kenny being killed anymore.
I've had some champagne now. I may be talking funny.
Forgive me.
It's early next morning.
The wind has settled down.
It's only in the 50s now.
The Animals' "House of the Rising Sun" is on repeat.
Maybe by accident, maybe not.
I can't get over the keyboard part
Then to see how stiff those dudes were when they played:
>   There is a house in New Orleans
>   They call The Rising Sun
>   And it's been the ruin of many a poor boy ...

In God he knew he won.
How's that?

They weren't soulful. Had never experienced pain
Enough to know how to move their bodies to the groove.
And why'd they have on suits.
Were they headed to a funeral?
Shoot, if a bitch just sold my new blue jeans I'd!
And if they was Girbaud or Guess ...
Well, she must be a bad, cigarette smoking hoarse-voiced sexy bitch.

Who just wants to kiss and fuck and not
Listen to all my bullshit. I had one once, in Jackson.
She left me. Moved to Asheville.
She read thick books and thought she was the shit.
Many were, but not her.
She was just a privileged bitch
Who liked to be choked and spit on.
I faked like I was cool.
Treated them all like shit so they'd stick around.
And they did, till someone *really* cool came along
Who played guitar and had an MFA.

As I reminisce I remember,
That some things weren't my fault.
Some things aren't anyone's fault.
Like if I'd died in this hurricane here
And left behind a bastard little baby boy.
A cute-ass, precious-ass lil' baby boy
Who may have grown up to be someone great
If only his dumbass father hadn't died
In a hurricane that The Weather Channel tracked for 6 weeks.
It wouldn't be mine, or even his fault.
Not at all. Because we chose to live
In this apartment, in this town
So close to the coast
And that I decided not to evacuate.
Wait, that's not entirely accurate.
We tried,
As a family, loaded up our most precious items:
Baby teeth, jewelry, snacks, clothes.
Made it to Orlando, well just outside it
Before traffic stopped moving altogether,
A bright red, undead, Jurassic snake.
The fear of running out of gas
And being stranded on the highway
Was real. As a family, we came home

The only ones on the road going south
And hunkered down, like oil rich hillbillies.

Maybe because we're lazy
Or maybe because we need
A good goddamn fight
To make us feel alive again
Every now and then, or what's the point?

It's not our fault,
We're dumb fucking humans who came from apes, right?

So it's never our fault, when you think about it.
And Matthew made me think about it.

If Dinosaurs Were Still Here

Outside my window, the grass sways
Gently as if some small critters are foraging.

Everyone will wake up soon
And the house will be buzzing with sound, movement.

If nothing matters (Metallica said it, they know)
Why did the dinosaurs go away?
Why did the dinosaurs go away?
If Ozzy and Keith Richards are still with us.

Today the Saints play Philly
Down in NOLA, the Superdome.
Yesterday saw Rams/Cowboys action.
Not sure who the winner was.
Over in Texas, footprints exist
Of man and dinosaur walking together.
Walking together, man and beast.
Who you think held the leash?

Over in Texas they got humongous French toast—
With real cane syrup, powdered sugar—
That no man or pregnant woman can finish.
It'll keep your motor running thru the long, exhausting day.
Hey, we don't all have access to adrenochrome.

So sweet, out the window
Between the jagged green palmetto things
Bugs flitter and flap their thin wings.
Somewhere out there a John Deere
Making much noise
Outside my home so early this morning.
Gears and grinding and scraping and mowing.

Raccoons rooting thru the recyclables
As I watch from behind my blinds.
Never do we shoo them away, but
The neighbors do, and say they full of rabies too.
They're more human than I thought.
Maybe charity ain't what's best for 'em afterall.

"Put a cinderblock on top of the can man," my neighbor said,
"That way they can't get in. You'd be doin' 'em
All kinds of favors there slick. By the way
Can I borrow your socket wrench for a couple days?"
"Sure, go right ahead."
"Is that your last Bud there in the cooler, I hate to ..."

"Go on ahead," I said. "There's more in my truck."
He took the beer, winked at me like Philip Marlowe to some rich whore
And walked towards his back porch.
I never heard the door shut
And the lawnmower sounds
Coming from the golf course faded
Like fragile, obsolete beliefs.

Sitting at the oak table in the kitchen
Looking out the window. Rain's coming,
Emancipator's playing, the lady and baby sleeping.
The sun slanting, as Faulkner used to say,
And I've seen it too: bright, cold and whitish gold goddammit.
The recollection of which is relentless and torturous.
Oh I've seen it by god, I didn't steal the image.
Seen it cut thru the living room of the house I grew up in
In the poorest town in the poorest state in the Union.

Bars, shafts of dusty sunlight cutting past the curtains.
Shedding brutal honesty, with divine precision
On every crack and stain and flaw it saw along the way.

Kinda counting the rings on the oak table
Kinda thinking, if the Saints win
They just need to win one more game and they're in the playoffs.
I'll win 40 bones from my homie and go
To Pete's Floristry up the street.
Walk out with a dozen or so roses
For some no-name fool in the cemetery
Who died too soon.
Before seeing what being a father means.
Before realizing we are infinite possibility.
If the Saints win the city will rejoice.
The city will rejoice in her diversity again (for a minute).

Then, in summer
The killings will begin.

The killings will begin again.
Tourists with fat wallets ("walking ATMs")
Will camp outside Anne Rice's house
In all black clothing, praying to the unknown.

So sweet tho, those beignets.
So sweet tho, State Palace Theatre raves.
So sweet tho, Willie Mae's fried chicken,
Boudin, crawfish pies and Miller Lite.

If the dinosaurs were still here, would we be?
I mean it, they were massive and had huge sharp teeth
Made for crushing bone and shredding meat.

"Naw," said someone behind me.
I'd asked the question out loud apparently.
"They were herbivores, dumbass.
Their teeth were made for shredding plants
Leaves and other nutritious, sunkissed greens.

Like most everything they get a bad rap
When really they was prolly a'ight.

If you know anything
Then you know it was a comet that killed 'em.
You should try to live better yourself
Before yo stank-ass goes extinct."

A moment of bewildered eye contact: "What's for breakfast dipshit?"

My old *buddy*, Bobby. Bobby Dee,
From Vtown, sat down at the table beside me.
Outta nowhere! Thin air.
Patted and rubbed his tummy
As he made fun of my old man haircut.
Was I looking at a ghost?
He was diagnosed with mesothelioma 10 years ago
So, I never figured on seeing him again.

After a plate of ham and eggs,
2 coffees and 3 mimosas
He told the most outrageous stories.
About Saudi women, wine, war.
And 'bout how he's ... lived more life than me.

Whirring Little Pretty Day
Gone Biddy Bye-Bye

The people
Who work next to me
Criticize us, in Dutch, Hebrew and Greek.
Makes me feel like I'm in a
Museum café
In some exotic, busy city
That at first I didn't want to visit
But grew to love/hate.
Like Havana/Hemingway.

To be a man
Is to always be boxing
Chin down, mouth shut.
Arrogance gone.

Before long
Apologies won't matter.
The art of time travel
Will be revealed to us
For our one good collective deed:
Trying to save all the little animals.
All the little animals trapped
In the untamable blaze.

The people
Working next to me
Are thinking about coffee, crepes,
Not the kid who got shot
Stealing a car out the parking lot
Of a local dealer recently.

God bless American fire fighters
Flying across the globe
To put out fires
And protect the little animals' homes.
Their fur is on fire goshdangit.
Their scales melting.

Kids of all colors
Beautiful children, and adults too
Who belong in the movies
Dying in the streets of Lake Worth,
West Palm and Riviera Beach.

The people working next to me
Have no idea
What happened last night.
Hit and runs.
Domestic violence.
Men murdering their wives.
Folks fighting for their next meal.
Folks fighting for their lives.

The pretty people
Who, no offense, sit next to me
And all day watch soccer on TV
Are from Morocco, the Antilles.
Foreigners, who don't care
About America
Eat Grand Slam breakfasts
With sausage, bacon and eggs.
Sipping coffee by the gallon,
Gossiping,
And kissing each other on the cheek over everything.

Work ended.
I was gone from there.

Beer in hand.
Gone from there.

At the house
Toys all over the floor.
Evidence of life being lived.
Child being loud:
Running screaming laughing punching us.
My nuts, Lucia's ass cheeks, wildly.
Not caring about anyone's feelings.
We love him for it.
One day we'll fight for real
And I'll win to teach him a valuable lesson.

Autoheart — "My Hallelujah" (Listening to it)
John Anderson — "Years" (Listen to it)

Time is all we got.
It's just us,
On this rock
Going around the sun.
That's all time is.
It's all we got.

Yes I'd like to fuck the younger you but she's gone.
She's gone.
The me, number 33
That scored 27 points, had 10 assists and 12 boards
Is gone.
Gone like your favorite swimming hole
Back home has dried up and been filled with garbage.
He's all worried now, thin-haired and scared
But not weak. Every boxing coach knows, power, is the last attribute to go.

I wanted to make the lady laugh.
I came home from work wanting to make her laugh.

For putting up with me
All these years.
She works hard, never complains.
Is a great mother,
And takes great pains to see to the comfort of others.
So after pounding a few Budweisers
I burped a stanky beer burp
In one of my unlaced Eastlands,
Had her come near (as if to whisper in her ear)
And stuck the fumes in her face.
Watched her suck them in (panic stricken).
To make her laugh.
To do something childish and stupid to get a laugh.

She didn't laugh.
Her eyes got big. White.
She yelled,
She screamed: "Never do that again!"
And was serious.

I crawfished into the kitchen,
A scolded dog.
This is bad my friend,

She's never mad.

Begin Again

~rmation can be obtained
~sting.com
~3A
~1211221
√00006B/244